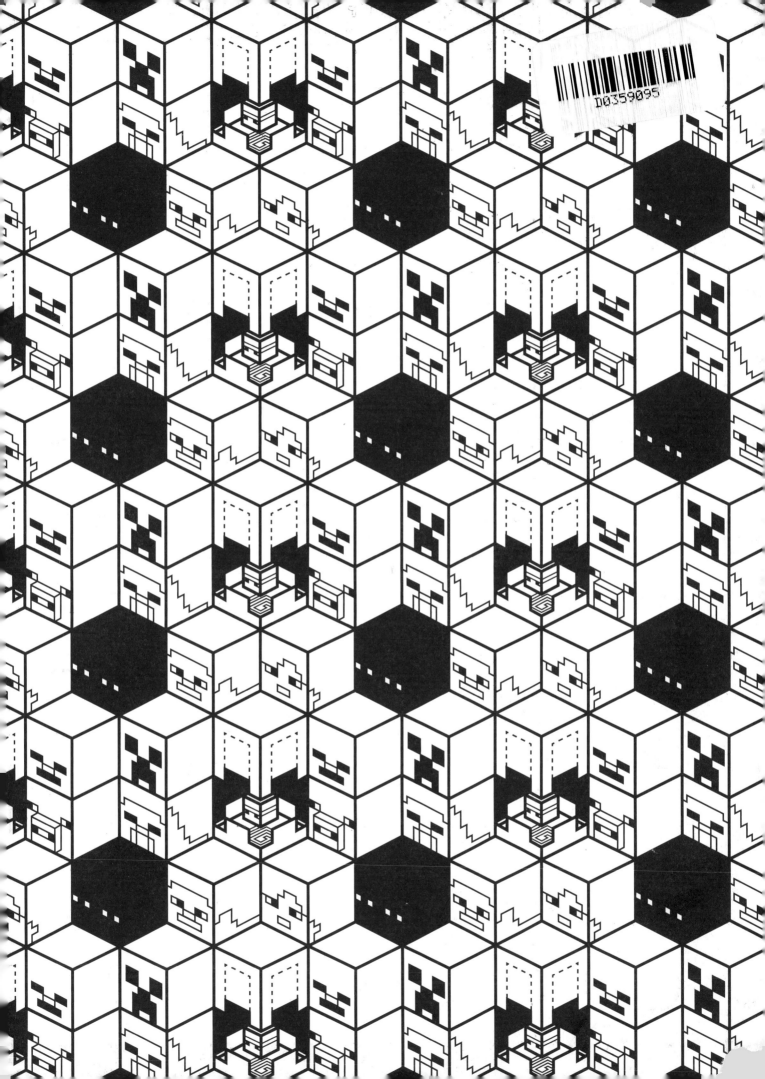

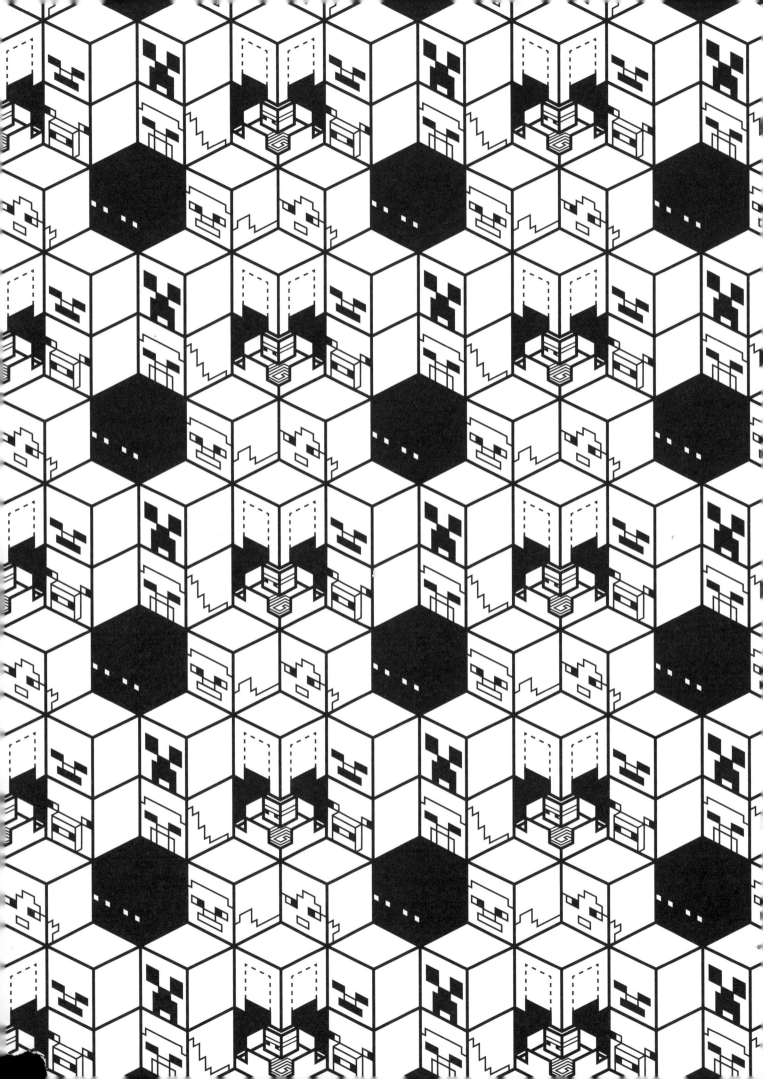

EGMONT

We bring stories to life

First published in Great Britain 2016 by Egmont UK Limited
The Yellow Building, 1 Nicholas Road, London W11 4AN

Written by Stephanie Milton.
Additional material by Owen Hill, Lydia Winters, Aleksandra Zajac, Shoghi Cervantes, Marc Watson,
Michael Stoyke, Erik Broes, Brynjólfur 'Binni' Erlingsson, Ninni Landin, Marsh Davies, Pontus Westerberg,
FyreUK, Joseph Garrett and Sarah Brown.
Illustrations by Joe McLaren, Ninni Landin and Ryan Marsh.
Designed by Mojang AB.
Cover designed by Joe Bolder.
Las Vegas MINECON photos © Mojang AB.
Florida MINECON photos © Mojang AB.
London MINECON photos © David Portass.
Block by Block photos © Mojang AB.
Production by Stef Fischetti and Laura Grundy.
Special thanks to Lydia Winters, Owen Hill, Junkboy, Martin Johansson,
Marsh Davies and Marc Watson.

MOJANG

ISBN 978 1 4052 8486 8

65708/1
Printed in the UK

ONLINE SAFETY FOR YOUNGER FANS

Spending time online is great fun! Here are a few simple rules to help younger fans
stay safe and keep the internet a great place to spend time:

- Never give out your real name – don't use it as your username.
- Never give out any of your personal details.
- Never tell anybody which school you go to or how old you are.
- Never tell anybody your password except a parent or a guardian.
- Be aware that you must be 13 or over to create an account on many sites. Always check
the site policy and ask a parent or guardian for permission before registering.
- Always tell a parent or guardian if something is worrying you.

Stay safe online. Any website addresses listed in this book are correct at the time of going to print. However,
Egmont is not responsible for content hosted by third parties. Please be aware that online content can be
subject to change and websites can contain content that is unsuitable for children.
We advise that all children are supervised when using the internet.

MINECRAFT™

MOJANG

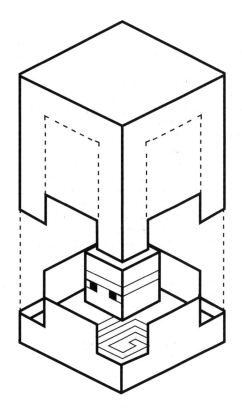

ANNUAL
2017

CONTENTS

HELLO!

Welcome to the Minecraft Annual 2017! Thanks for purchasing this or, if you got it as a gift from a friend or family member, thanks for making it clear that you like Minecraft enough to read 72 pages about it! There are loads of great books around, so we really appreciate you opening up this one.

It's been a busy year for all things Minecraft – we've released new editions of the game, updated the older ones, and hosted the biggest MINECON yet. By the time you're reading this, there's a chance that Minecraft: Education Edition is being used to teach students in a school near you, and that Block by Block – our collaborative project with UN-Habitat – is giving more people around the world a chance to redesign their surroundings. We're extremely proud of what Minecraft has become over the past few years.

We've tried to pack this annual with a little bit of all things Minecrafty. Some parts are designed to help you become a better player, some might inspire exciting builds, and some provide fun facts and insight into our amazing community. We hope you enjoy all of it!

Thanks for playing.

Owen Hill,
Mojang

MINECRAFT TIMELINE

2009

NOTCH AND THE BIRTH OF MINECRAFT

Notch begins working on his game idea, and quits his job so that he can concentrate on it full-time. At first he calls it 'Cave Game' but later, when he releases the first version to the public, he officially changes the name to Minecraft.

An early screenshot of a Minecraft landscape, when the world was a simpler, quieter place.

THE EVOLUTION OF MINECRAFT

After initial development Minecraft moves to Survival Test where creepers are introduced. It then moves into In Development stage so that the community can try out new features, including crafting, furnaces and torches.

Survival evolves quickly in the early development stages – creepers were the first mob added in Survival Test.

2009 HIGHLIGHTS
- The first Minecraft accounts are registered
- The official Minecraft forum opens

2010

NEW ADDITIONS TO THE GAME

Minecarts are added, giving players the opportunity to build minecart systems and travel more quickly. Redstone is also added, giving the community the power to create switches for things like doors. The Nether is also introduced.

Minecart systems allow players to travel long distances more quickly, and transport items.

The power of redstone – players are now able to build doors with switches to keep unwelcome visitors out.

COMMUNITY GROWTH AND GAME RECOGNITION

A spontaneous gathering of fifty Minecrafters – called 'Minecraftcon' – takes place in Washington State after Notch posted a request for a meet-up via an online blog post. Minecraft is awarded indie game of the year by IndieDB.

2010 HIGHLIGHTS
- Multiplayer is officially released
- Minecraft reaches 100,000 registered users
- Mojang AB is officially founded

2011

US gamer Kurt J Mac, the man who bravely set out on a quest for Minecraft's far lands.

KURT J MAC SETS OUT FOR THE FAR LANDS

US gamer Kurt J Mac sets out on a journey to find the edge of Minecraft. Three years later, he calculates that he's walked a total of 1,479,940 blocks from his original spawn point and raised over $335,000 for Child's Play Charity.

NEW ADDITIONS TO THE GAME

The Adventure Update is released, adding endermen, silverfish and cave spiders, as well as villages, strongholds and abandoned mineshafts. Minecraft's first boss mob, the ender dragon, is officially added to the game.

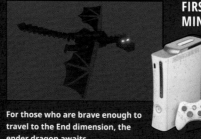

For those who are brave enough to travel to the End dimension, the ender dragon awaits ...

2011 HIGHLIGHTS
- Minecraft is officially out of Beta
- Minecraft passes 10 million registered users
- Minecraft Pocket Edition is released for Android
- Jeb becomes lead developer

2012

NEW ADDITIONS TO THE GAME

The jungle biome is added to Minecraft, bringing with it ocelots and cats, as well as iron golems. The Pretty Scary Update is released in October, adding witches, bats, zombie villagers, wither skeletons and a second boss mob, the wither.

A whole host of mobs are added to Minecraft in 2012, but the wither boss has got to be the scariest ...

FIRST OFFICIAL LEGO SET IS RELEASED

LEGO announce their intention to create official Minecraft sets after they get the required number of votes. In February they reveal the final design of the very first set, 'Micro World', and the final product is released in June.

FIRST CONSOLE EDITION OF MINECRAFT RELEASED

The first ever console edition of Minecraft is released for Xbox 360. In the first 24 hours after release it sells 400,000 copies. The first skin packs are released over the course of the year.

2012 HIGHLIGHTS
- Minecraft is released for Xbox 360
- On Christmas Eve alone, Minecraft sells 453,000 copies across all platforms

Minecraft has come a long way since its birth in 2009, and it currently has over 100 million registered users worldwide. This year-by-year timeline shows some of the most exciting developments in the life of the game, alongside a few of the community's most amazing achievements.

2013

REDSTONE AND HORSE UPDATES

The Redstone Update introduces several new blocks, including activator rails, daylight sensors, comparators, trapped chests and weighted pressure plates. Horses, horse armour and hay blocks are added in The Horse Update.

2013 was a good year for transport in Minecraft, with the addition of both activator rails and horses.

THE UPDATE THAT CHANGED THE WORLD

The Update That Changed the World introduces several new biomes including mesa, flower forest and deep ocean. It also introduces two new tree types (acacia and dark oak) and three new fish, as well as stained glass and red sand.

The landscape of Minecraft looks quite different now, with exciting new biomes to explore.

2013 HIGHLIGHTS

- Minecraft is released for PlayStation 3
- Minecraft sales hit 13 million for PC/Mac Edition

2014

THE COUNTRY OF DENMARK IS BUILT IN MINECRAFT

The Danish Geodata Agency makes the first ever model of an entire country in a video game in April, revealing their 1:1 scale build of Denmark. They recreated every single building and feature – that's 43,000 square kilometres in total.

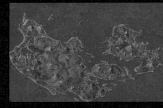

This map of Denmark comes to around a terabyte of data in total and is made of almost four billion blocks.

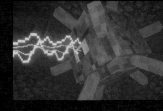

The ocean monuments, introduced during The Bountiful Update, are full of guardians and elder guardians.

NEW ADDITIONS TO THE GAME

The Bountiful Update adds new types of stone, banners, slime and barrier blocks as well as rabbits and ocean monuments. A new default skin, Alex, is added.

2014 HIGHLIGHTS

- Minecraft is released for PlayStation Vita, Xbox One and PlayStation 4
- Minecraft reaches 100 million registered users
- Realms is launched worldwide

2015

Joseph Kelly with his certificate after breaking the world record for longest Minecraft marathon.

JOSEPH KELLY SMASHES WORLD RECORD

UK gamer Joseph Kelly smashes the world record for the longest Minecraft marathon in October 2015. It lasted 35 hours, 35 minutes and 35 seconds on the PC/Mac Edition, and he raised £1,800 for Cancer Research in the process.

EPISODE 1 OF MINECRAFT: STORY MODE IS RELEASED

The first episode of Minecraft: Story Mode, the episodic spin-off game created by Telltale Games, is released for PC/Mac, Xbox and PlayStation consoles and iOS, Android and Fire OS. This is shortly followed by episodes 2, 3 and 4.

Jesse and the gang, the lead characters in Minecraft: Story Mode, begin their epic adventure in the first episode.

2015 HIGHLIGHTS

- Minecraft sales hit 20 million for PC/Mac Edition
- Minecraft is released for Wii U and Windows 10

2016

STORY MODE RECOGNITION AND UPDATES

Episode 1 of Story Mode is released for Wii U. Story Mode is nominated for a Kids' Choice Award for Favourite Video Game. Episode 5 of Story Mode is released. Telltale confirm that 3 more episodes will follow later in 2016.

Episode 5 of Story Mode – 'Order Up!'. The adventure continues as Jesse and the gang head to an abandoned temple.

NEW ADDITIONS TO THE GAME

The Combat Update is released. New additions include dual wielding, tipped arrows and shields. Combat in the End dimension becomes more difficult, and End cities are added, bringing with them elytra and hostile shulkers.

MINECRAFT: EDUCATION EDITION EARLY ACCESS

The early access programme for Minecraft: Education Edition is released in June, for teachers to try out for free. When it officially launches it will be available in 11 languages and 41 countries.

2016 HIGHLIGHTS

- The MineCon 2016 announcement trailer is released – MineCon will be held in Anaheim, California
- The new and improved Minecraft website, Minecraft.net, launches

BEST AND WORST DAYS IN MINECRAFT: MOJANG EDITION

Everyone at Mojang loves playing Minecraft, and between them there's no shortage of best day memories. But, just like the rest of us, they've had some bad days, too. Here, for the first time, Lydia, Marc and Ninni reveal their best and worst days.

THE BRAND DIRECTOR

LYDIA WINTERS

BEST DAY When I started playing Minecraft in Alpha, I knew that finding a diamond was one of the best things you could do in the game. I searched high and low, visited different caves, but no matter where I went I wasn't finding a diamond, or I was dying before I could dig down deep enough. When I finally saw those turquoise, glittering flecks of diamond ore, all the new things I'd be able to make flashed in my mind. That was my best moment!

WORST DAY When wolves were first added to the game I searched everywhere to find one for myself. I killed lots of skeletons and collected their bones so that I would be able to tame a wolf as soon as I found one. Then the moment finally came and I found not one, but THREE wolves at once. Unfortunately, in my extreme excitement, I hit one of the wolves with a bone instead of feeding it. Noooooo. All three wolves became hostile and attacked me, and I had to kill them to defend myself. No wolf pet for me.

THE REALMS CONTENT MANAGER

MARC WATSON

BEST DAY My friends and I started a new server. We marked out a hill, and minutes later it was flattened. We decided where the farm would go, and soon after we had a flourishing farm. We stayed online and chatted for hours, gathering and sharing resources and building our new town together.

WORST DAY Shortly after I started playing, I died at the hands of a skeleton in a cave, leaving everything I had collected so far in a pile on the ground. I returned to fight that skeleton nearly a dozen times, but eventually the items disappeared. Defeated, I made my way home, where the sun was rising. A flaming zombie wandered onto the bridge to my house and burned it down.

THE ARTIST

NINNI LANDIN

BEST DAY I built a gigantic rollercoaster made of glass surrounding my base in Survival mode. It was my first redstone project and it was a lot of fun to explore all of its possibilities – from powered rails to ways of storing and ejecting carts. It took three days but it was completely worth the effort.

WORST DAY A friend and I decided to explore the Nether fortress for the first time. We found awesome loot among hostile blazes which nearly killed us. We escaped and came up with the clever idea that we needed a base inside the fortress, with a bed down there in case we died. Little did we know that beds explode when you try to sleep in them in the Nether ...

STAMPY'S HOT BUNS

Stampy's Hot Buns is the bakery in Stampy's Lovely World that provides all his friends with delicious cake and bread. Take a look at the picture on this page to see how it's built, then turn the page to see how to get the details right so you can recreate it in your own world.

ㄹ: ROOF

The roof of Stampy's Hot Buns is made out of snow. It looks just like icing on top of a cake.

1: WALLS

Stampy wanted the bakery to look like a real, solid building, but also a bit like a cake, so he's made the walls out of wood logs.

Stampys hot buns.

ヨ: SIGNS AND ITEM FRAMES

A sign above the door lets visitors know they've arrived at Stampy's Hot Buns. He's also placed two item frames next to the sign, containing cake and bread, to entice customers inside. Yum!

THIS IS STAMPY

Stampy Cat is a YouTuber who loves to play Minecraft on his Xbox 360. He has spent over 200 hours in his Lovely World, building, playing games and having fun with his friends. He has added 500 people to the Love Garden in his Lovely World, including Mojang and 4J Studios, and he currently has 10 pet dogs that he takes on his adventures with him. Over 7 million people have subscribed to his channel.

youtube.com/stampycat

STAMPY'S HOT BUNS

🕒 45 MINS ❶❷③④ EASY

1: CAKE AND BREAD DISPLAY

Stampy's Hot Buns is packed with shelves full of delicious cakes for customers to choose from. Stampy's friends helped him make shelves using fences and wood slabs. There are also several chests full of bread in the middle of the bakery floor.

2: GARDEN

Stampy's bakery is completely self-sufficient – there's a garden outside which is split into a crop farm and an animal enclosure. He grows sugar cane and wheat, and breeds cows and chickens so he has everything he needs.

3: FLOOR

The floor of Stampy's Hot Buns is made from alternating blocks of glowstone and snow. Stampy wanted his bakery to be light and fun, and this floor is much less boring than plain old wood planks.

4: TILL AND KITCHEN AREA

There's a till area next to the door where Stampy's customers can pay for their purchases. The till is made from a wood stair block, and there's also a minecart behind the counter for the server to sit in. The kitchen area next to the till is where Stampy makes his cakes and bread. It contains furnaces and a crafting table, as well as a large chest full of ingredients laid out in the shape of a smiley face!

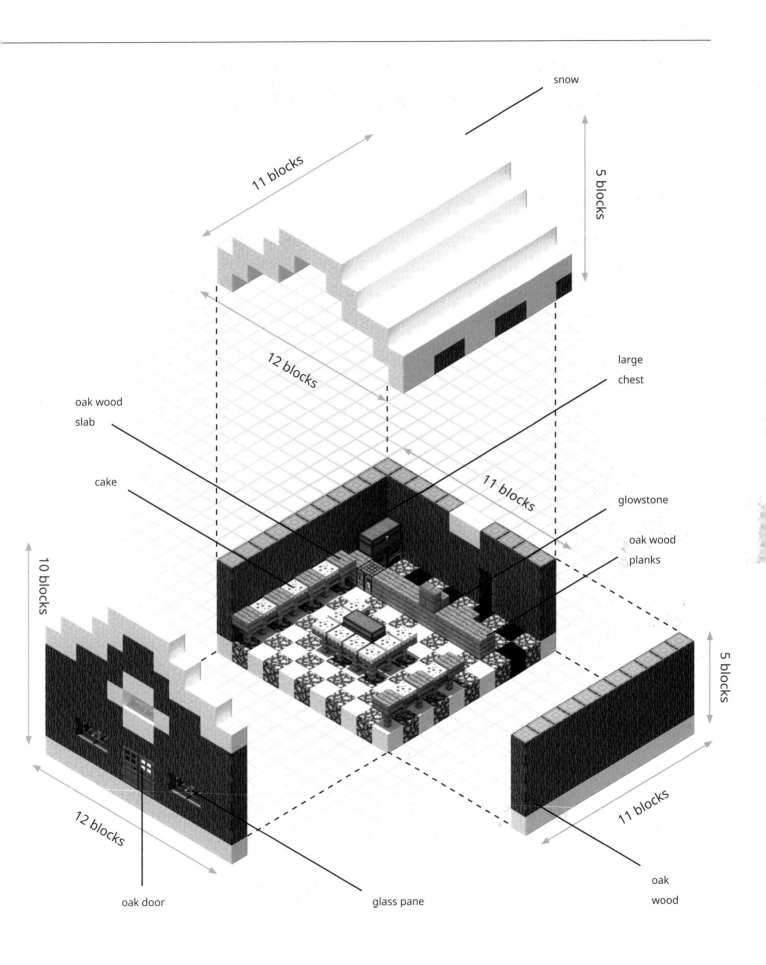

snow

11 blocks

5 blocks

12 blocks

large
chest

oak wood
slab

11 blocks

cake

glowstone

oak wood
planks

10 blocks

5 blocks

12 blocks

11 blocks

oak door

glass pane

oak
wood

MINECRAFT CHALLENGES: MOJANG EDITION

Looking for some fun challenge ideas to try out next time you play Minecraft? From redstone challenges to playing in 'vampire mode', the Mojang team really know how to make things interesting. Check out their ideas below and give them a go next time you play.

THE BRAND DIRECTOR

LYDIA WINTERS

Have you ever raced to see how quickly you can find a diamond? Gather a few friends together and challenge them to see who can find a diamond first, then bring it back to a specific spot. Or try it at home a few times and see if you can beat your own record time.

THE GAME DEVELOPER

MICHAEL STOYKE

My challenge is a redstone challenge: try to use ten pistons on each other and build redstone around it so that it works like an elevator. You'll need to make it travel up and down.

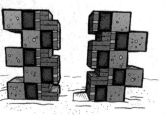

THE PROJECT MANAGER

ALEKSANDRA ZAJAC

I love to watch Minecraft Ultra Hardcore Survival Games on YouTube – it's a great challenge. There's no health regeneration and potions are limited. It brings players back to basic, day-to-day survival: gathering supplies and food in order to survive the night in caves, fighting monsters and looking for ores. Creating armour, weapons, using enchantments or venturing to the Nether will bring them closer to victory.

The first few days are stressful since you're forced to act as fast as you can and gather as many apples as possible. Every night brings fear and danger. Then you relax when the initial hype fades. Finally there is a moment of truth, where only a few players are left on the map and the adrenaline hits. There can only be one winner!

THE DATA WAREHOUSE MANAGER

BRYNJÓLFUR 'BINNI' ERLINGSSON

 Try playing in 'vampire mode' – you're not allowed to come into contact with sunlight. Dig yourself underground and build your house in a cave. You can only come out at night, when the world is a much more dangerous place.

THE GAME DEVELOPER

ERIK BROES

 Build a tower as high as you can, take a bucket of water and then jump off the tower. Before you land, try to place the bucket of water underneath you so that it breaks your fall.

THE GAME DEVELOPER

SHOGHI CERVANTES

 Spawn in superflat and try to survive by locating villages and killing slimes. Wood will be scarce, until you find saplings in a chest. Zombies will assault the villages every night. You'll have to trade for tools or find ingots in chests, and find a village with a lava source so you can create a Nether portal. It isn't possible to fight the dragon here, but you can fight the wither and get a beacon.

THE ARTIST

NINNI LANDIN

 I love to explore new territory and build new bases and villages, but the distance between them all is pretty far. My goal is to connect all of my key points to

an enormous subway system with stations and all. Why don't you try it out, too?

MINECRAFT REALMS

Playing Minecraft with other people over the internet is a lot of fun, but it can be tricky to set up. Which is why Mojang created Realms – a service that allows you to set up an online world which can be accessed by an approved list of up to two hundred players.

THE TECHNICAL STUFF

One person will need to subscribe and host the Realm, but once it's set up this person doesn't need to be logged in for the other players to be able to access the world. Realms is completely secure, and your worlds are automatically backed up so you can restore them to a previously saved point whenever you need to.

Visit minecraft.net/realms and follow the instructions to set up for PC/Mac Edition. Realms will be available for other editions of Minecraft soon.

THE FUN STUFF

OK, enough with the technical talk. Let's get to the fun stuff – what can you actually do on Realms? Well, you have a few options: you can start from a random seed and see what kind of cool spawn you get, you can replace your regular world with an adventure map, or you can temporarily replace it with a minigame. Turn the page to get a taste of the excitement that awaits.

MINECRAFT REALMS

Here's some of the best Realms content created by the talented Minecraft community.

DRAGNOZ, SAMASAURUS6 AND BLOCKWORKS

WE ARE THE RANGERS

In this adventure map you're a ranger who must protect the animals from the hostile mobs and poachers who pose a threat to them. The custom animals include lions, elephants and zebras. It's designed to raise awareness of the real threat posed to wildlife around the world, particularly from poachers.

DRAGNOZ

RANDOM SKIES

This is a randomly generated survival parkour map. Your objective is to survive and complete the list of challenges as quickly as you can.

TEAM WOOLOO

TOTAL HOUSE BOMBOVER

If you like blowing things up, this is the map for you. The aim is to blow up the entire house using the TNT given to you.

TEAM WOOLOO

HALF HEART RACE

In this minigame you have to manoeuvre your way through a tricky parkour map with only two hearts and no regeneration. You can race the clock or your friends.

The entire Half Heart Race map is fraught with peril, especially the Nether-themed sections.

SLICEDLIME

BUILD-OFF PARKOUR

In this minigame you can choose to add three blocks of your choice to the parkour map or try to play it as it is. Once you start to play, all the white blocks will disappear.

If chosen and placed wisely, three blocks can make all the difference in Build-off Parkour.

SPINDLEWOOD

Spindlewood is a dark, gothic-style survival map crawling with hostile mobs and haunted by Japanese spirits.

A TREEMENDOUS SPAWN

In this map you'll spawn right by an enormous treehouse. The surrounding area is decorated with large, colourful flowers.

NOBLEMAN, VEK AND PAAAAAAAT

DESERT NOOK

This desert-themed survival spawn features a custom desert temple, a village and the beginnings of a minecart system.

BLOCKWORKS

WINTER STRONGHOLD

This is an adventure map with a difference. Instead of starting at a random spawn you start inside a stronghold complete with supplies.

Halfway through a competitive game of Carrot Catcher, the field is likely to look something like this.

GEMOZ

CARROT CATCHER

This minigame is simple yet fun. You'll be dropped into the middle of an enormous field of carrots, and the object of the game is to harvest 1000 carrots before your opponent does. Fun power-ups appear as you play – some inflict the levitation effect on all other players or send hungry rabbits over to sabotage their harvesting efforts, others teleport all nearby carrots over to you or refill the entire field with carrots.

BLOCK BY BLOCK

Block by Block is a partnership between Mojang and the United Nations Human Settlements Programme (UN-Habitat), the UN agency working towards a better urban future by promoting sustainable towns and cities.

The UN recognises how important it is for everyone to have access to safe public space. The goal of Block by Block is to support UN-Habitat's Global Public Space Programme to improve public spaces worldwide.

Block by Block involves people, particularly youth, women and slum residents, in the reconstruction plans for their own neighbourhoods, giving them the opportunity to show planners how they would like their local public spaces to look. It can be difficult to get citizens involved in processes like this, and Minecraft has turned out to be the perfect tool to encourage them to make their voices heard and contribute their ideas.

Visit blockbyblock.org to find out more.

BLOCK BY BLOCK LOCATIONS

Through the Block by Block initiative, Minecraft is quite literally changing the world. From Mexico City, Mexico to Mumbai, India, projects are taking place on every continent to improve public spaces. This world map shows projects which are currently in progress or have been completed.

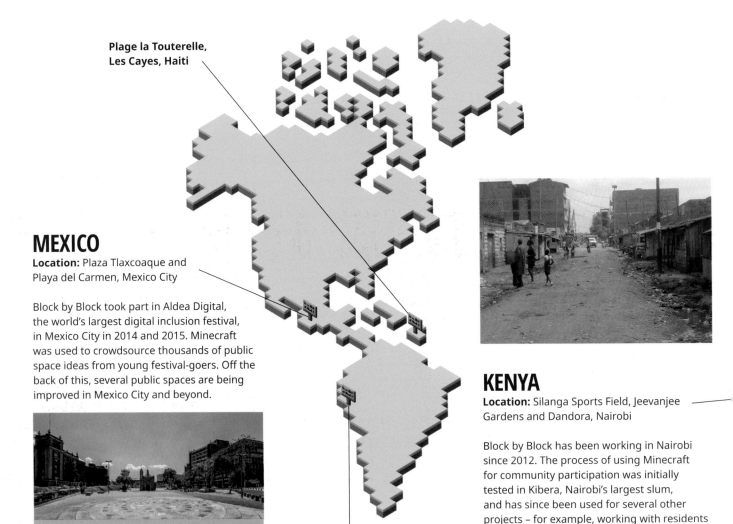

Plage la Touterelle,
Les Cayes, Haiti

MEXICO

Location: Plaza Tlaxcoaque and Playa del Carmen, Mexico City

Block by Block took part in Aldea Digital, the world's largest digital inclusion festival, in Mexico City in 2014 and 2015. Minecraft was used to crowdsource thousands of public space ideas from young festival-goers. Off the back of this, several public spaces are being improved in Mexico City and beyond.

Villa el Salvador,
Lima, Peru

KENYA

Location: Silanga Sports Field, Jeevanjee Gardens and Dandora, Nairobi

Block by Block has been working in Nairobi since 2012. The process of using Minecraft for community participation was initially tested in Kibera, Nairobi's largest slum, and has since been used for several other projects – for example, working with residents of the Dandora slum to redesign their neighbourhood in 2015. Block by Block is also helping the Nairobi local government improve sixty public spaces across the city.

KOSOVO

Location: Sunny Hill, Pristina

Block by Block is improving two public spaces in Kosovo: one in the capital Pristina and one in the ethnically-divided northern city of Mitrovica. A Minecraft workshop was held in Pristina in September 2015, giving sixty young people the opportunity to design a public space in the Sunny Hill area of the city.

Preparanda Square, Lokoja, Nigeria

Dey Phuku, Kirtipur, Nepal

Solar Park, Khulna, Bangladesh

Rizal Park, Manila, Philippines

Multi-purpose field, Honiara, Solomon Islands

Sinay Market, Mogadishu, Somalia

End Street North Park, Johannesburg, South Africa

INDIA

Location: Gautam Nagar, Mumbai

In 2013 Block by Block improved Lotus Garden – a public space in M Ward, one of the poorest areas of Mumbai. Lotus Garden is one of the only dedicated public spaces in an area with a population of 200,000 people. Work has now started to improve public spaces around Gautam Nagar, a 'vertical slum' in the same area, and a Minecraft workshop was held in April 2016.

AMYLEE33'S GINGERBREAD TEA HOUSE

Everything in Amy's Land of Love is just lovely. All of her builds have been made with love and imagination, and her gingerbread tea house looks good enough to eat. Let's take a look at how Amy built it, so you can recreate it in your own Minecraft world, and perhaps invite her round for tea!

1: WALLS AND ROOF

Amy uses orange and pink wool to make the house look like it's made from gingerbread and cake, and white wool for an icing roof.

2: GIANT CANDY CANES

Two giant candy canes sit either side of the front door to Amy's gingerbread tea house. They have been made from alternating blocks of red and white wool.

3: CAKES

Amy's placed stacks of cake blocks against the outside walls. If Stampy ever comes round for a visit she'll have to keep a very close eye on him, or she isn't going to have any house left!

4: CHOCOLATE LAKE

Amy's used brown wool to create a chocolate lake and added a wooden water wheel to keep the chocolate flowing. Making things look round can be tricky in Minecraft, but gradually staggering wood blocks and using upside-down stair blocks will give you a realistic wheel.

THIS IS AMYLEE33

AmyLee33 loves to play Minecraft on her PC and make lovely videos for her YouTube channel. Amy's Land of Love is home to 9 dogs and 3 snow golems, and, in the 2 years she's been playing, she's never lost a dog. She has respawned 13 times and walked the equivalent of over 700 kilometres. As well as generally being lovely, she's also won over 1000 battles with monsters. Her channel has over 886,000 subscribers.

youtube.com/amyleethirty3

AMYLEE33'S GINGERBREAD TEA HOUSE

🕑 25 MINS **1 2** 3 4 EASY

1: CAKE CAFE

Pink and white wool have been used to create a cafe-style chequered floor, and sandstone blocks for white chocolate stairs.

2: TEA PARTY AREA

Amy sells cakes and hosts tea parties upstairs. There are lots of lovely pink tables, with flowers and cakes, and chairs made from wood stairs.

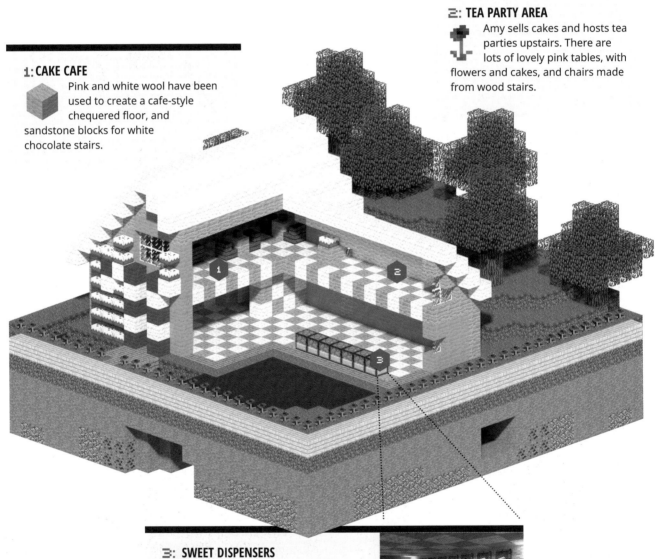

3: SWEET DISPENSERS

On the ground floor of the tea house there are lots of sweet dispensers for you to choose from, containing everything from white chocolate bars to sherbet.

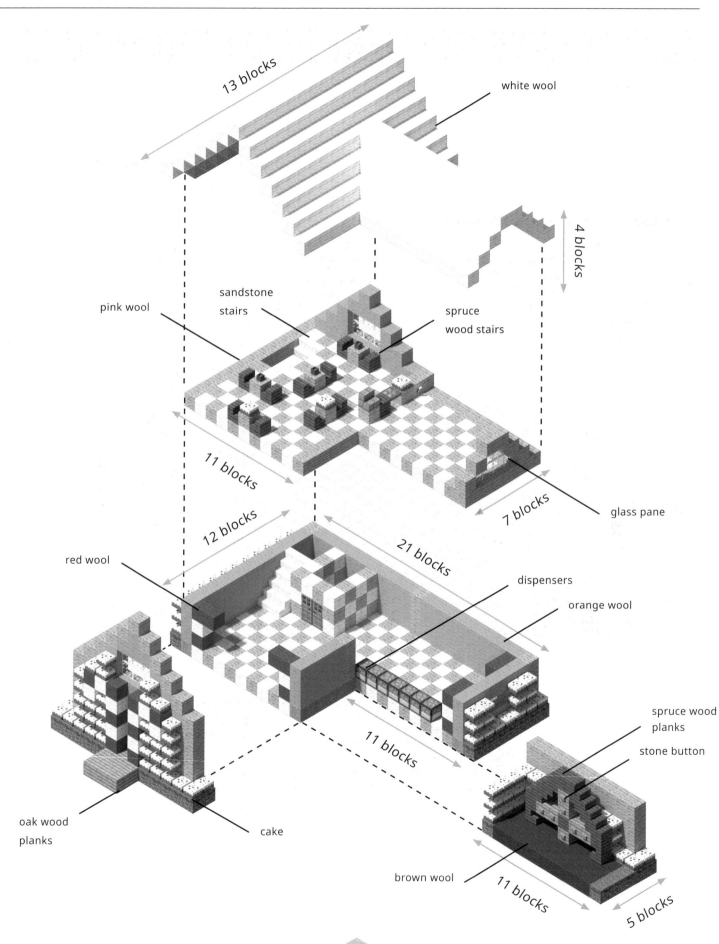

13 blocks

white wool

4 blocks

pink wool

sandstone stairs

spruce wood stairs

11 blocks

7 blocks

glass pane

12 blocks

21 blocks

red wool

dispensers

orange wool

11 blocks

spruce wood planks

stone button

oak wood planks

cake

brown wool

11 blocks

5 blocks

MINECRAFT CHALLENGES: YOUTUBER EDITION

The Minecraft YouTube community are very good at thinking up new and entertaining challenges to make their videos even more fun to create, and to watch. Stampy Cat, AmyLee33 and creative build team FyreUK have set some challenges for you to try next time you play. Have fun!

YOUTUBE.COM/FYREUK

FYREUK

Build a spacious, functional house in Survival mode, using only quartz, red wool and stone, and maybe some glass for windows, too. Include bedrooms, a kitchen, a living area and a staircase up to an upper floor. You could also build a fireplace out of netherrack. For even more of a challenge, build the entire house on a floating island suspended in mid-air.

Your finished house should be unique to look at and fairly regal, if you can pull it off ...

You could use the same blocks to create a palace, spaceship or coliseum instead. It's always a fun challenge to limit the blocks you use and see what you can come up with. Experiment enough and you might even find a favourite new style and theme that you can try out for future builds.

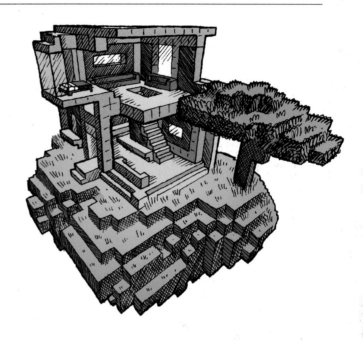

YOUTUBE.COM/AMYLEETHIRTY3

AMYLEE33

Here are some imaginative build challenges for you to try!

- Build a secret laboratory
- Build a huge treehouse
- Build a park for your dogs to have fun in
- Build a rollercoaster
- Build a racing track using minecarts and rails, then race your friends
- Invent something new!

YOUTUBE.COM/STAMPYCAT

STAMPY CAT

I challenge you to try the Backwards Challenge! You'll need to be playing in reverse third person view (switch your view twice), in Survival mode, in a new world. The challenge is to collect all the ingredients needed to make a cake whilst in this view – that's eggs, wheat, milk and sugar. You can only see behind you so it's harder than it sounds. Good luck!

NETHER CHALLENGE PART 1

Are you a pro Nether explorer looking for a new challenge? Repurposing a Nether fortress for your own use is the perfect way to test yourself in Survival and own Minecraft's most hellish dimension. Let's start by making the exterior safer and add some useful features.

1: NETHER PORTAL

Build an on-site portal, so you can run back and forth to the Overworld to collect materials that aren't available in the Nether (food, wood etc). Build it on a bridge and enclose it in cobblestone to protect it from ghast fireballs. Just make sure there isn't a 5 x 4 x 5 block space within the enclosure, as ghasts might spawn inside it.

2: BRIDGES

The bridges leading into the fortress are usually damaged, and it can be hard to spot holes in the dim light; taking time to repair them with Nether brick now will stop you falling through the gaps and into lava. Find an area of fortress that you're happy to sacrifice and mine it for the Nether brick you need for repairs.

▆: ENTRANCE SECURITY

You don't want mobs finding their way into the fortress when you're not looking, so add iron doors and switches to all entrances to the main building. That'll keep them out.

▜: GHAST SNIPER TURRET

Ghasts are one of the most dangerous Nether mobs – they spit fire charges and can target you from up to 100 blocks away. Build sniper turrets from Nether brick on each side of the fortress so you can shoot at them from a higher vantage point. Equip them with chests full of arrows, spare bows, enchanted golden apples and potions of healing and fire resistance.

▙: LAVA STREAMS

You'll need to block off all lava streams that intersect with the fortress. This can be tricky as many of them start right up in the Nether ceiling. Use dirt blocks to carefully tower your way up, then block off the streams with cobblestone. If that's too difficult, use blocks to divert the flow away from the fortress lower down instead.

NETHER CHALLENGE PART 2

Once you've secured the exterior you can move inside the fortress and really make yourself at home. There are a few hazards you'll need to deal with to make it safe enough to live in, and you'll also need to kit it out with supplies so that you can survive in there long-term.

1: LIGHT

 Use torches, glowstone and jack o'lanterns to light up the fortress. This will stop wither skeletons from spawning as the light level needs to be seven or lower.

3: EQUIPMENT

Find a secure location within the main building to set up your equipment – ideally a crafting table, furnace, chest of supplies, ender chest to link back to the Overworld and equipment for brewing potions. Don't be tempted to add a bed – it'll explode if you try to sleep in it.

2: INTERNAL SECURITY

Replacing the fortress floors with slab blocks or transparent blocks will prevent mobs from spawning. If this isn't possible make sure you're always on the lookout for mobs, especially magma cubes and zombie pigmen which can spawn at any light level. Always have your enchanted diamond sword and bow ready.

4: BLAZE SPAWNERS

You could try to disable the blaze spawners using torches or glowstone, but since the light level will need to be 11 or higher this usually doesn't work. Instead, encase them in a 12 x 12 x 12 cobblestone or glass enclosure. Blazes will spawn up to 4 blocks away from the spawner and a block above or below it, so they'll be trapped inside the enclosure and won't be a threat to you.

SPARRENHOUT

Sparrenhout is a survival spawn available through Realms. 'Sparrenhout' means 'spruce wood' in Dutch, and it's not difficult to see how the creator Springstof decided on the name – you spawn next to a charming cottage in the middle of a spruce forest.

1: SPRUCE FOREST

The cottage is set in a peaceful glade in the middle of the spruce forest. The dense tree cover provides an excellent source of wood and hides some interesting features that you can explore when you're more familiar with your surroundings.

2: COTTAGE GROUNDS

Just outside the front door of the cottage you'll find several crafting tables, a chest, a furnace, an anvil and several blocks of hay. That's everything you need to get crafting and stock the cottage full of supplies.

∃: COTTAGE EXTERIOR

The cottage has been built from wood and stone so it blends into the forest. Smaller details have been created using trapdoors, stone buttons, cauldrons and leaf blocks.

SPARRENHOUT

Inside the cottage you'll find a safe, comfortable environment, thoughtfully filled with supplies and equipment to keep you safe. Take a look at this cutaway of the cottage interior, then use the exploded diagram opposite to help you recreate it in your own Minecraft world.

1 Hour **1 2 3** MEDIUM

1: SEATING AREA

A comfortable seating area welcomes you into the cottage. There's even a blue orchid in a flower pot.

2: SECOND FLOOR

On the second floor you'll find everything you need to help you relax after a hard day: a bed, bookshelves, and even an armour stand.

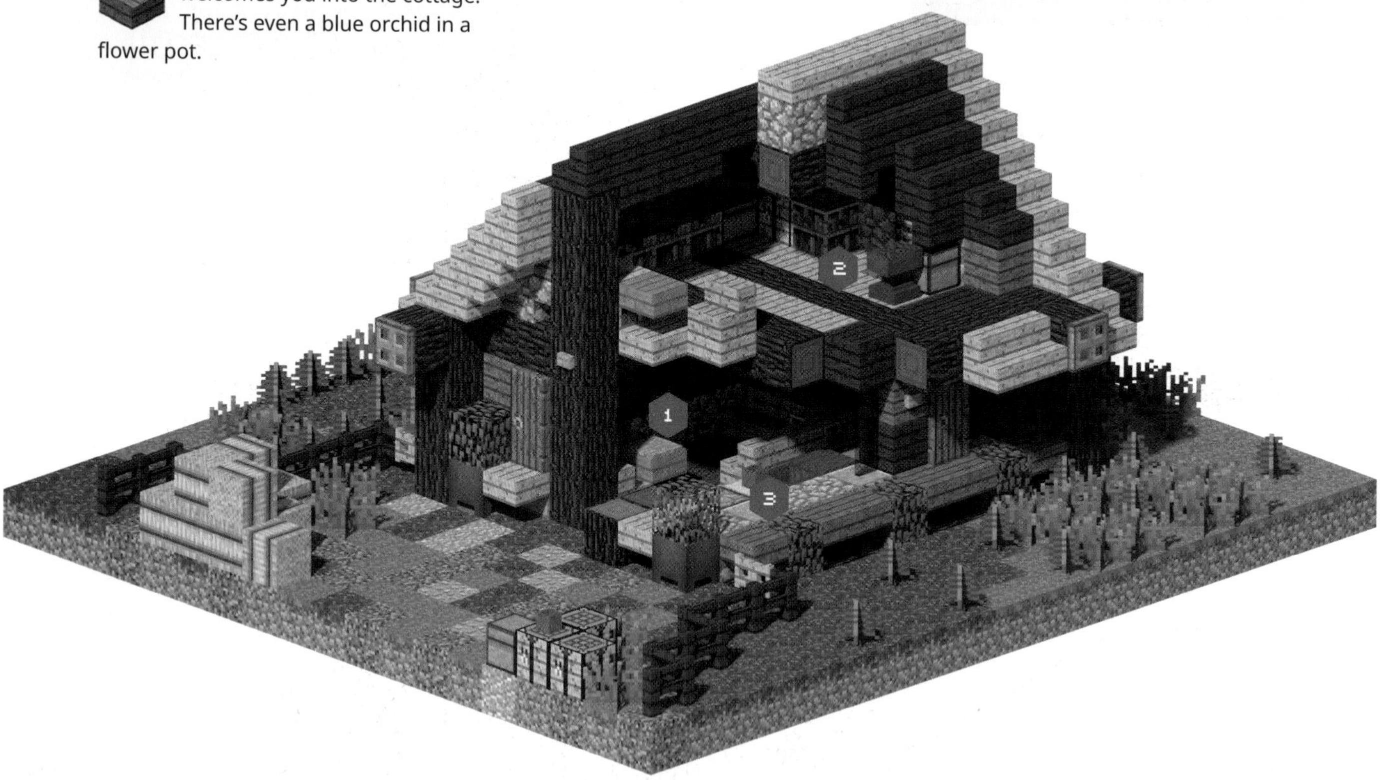

3: EQUIPMENT

You'll find more equipment inside, including a crafting table, a furnace and a chest that has been filled with a variety of food items.

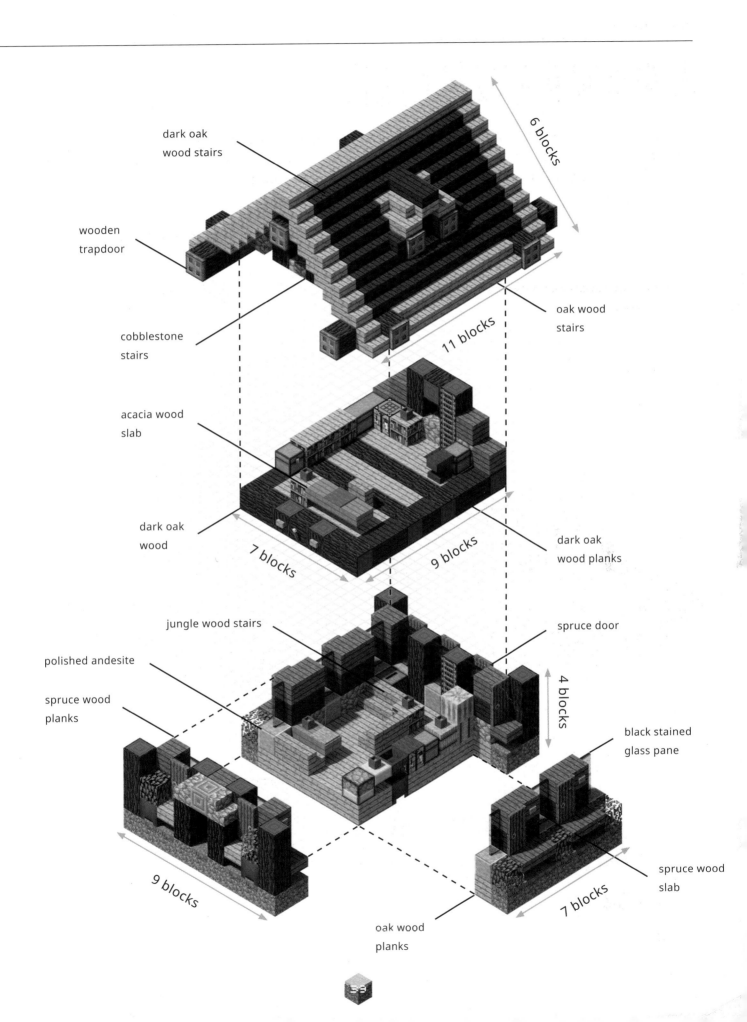

dark oak
wood stairs

wooden
trapdoor

cobblestone
stairs

acacia wood
slab

dark oak
wood

jungle wood stairs

polished andesite

spruce wood
planks

6 blocks

11 blocks

oak wood
stairs

7 blocks

9 blocks

dark oak
wood planks

spruce door

4 blocks

black stained
glass pane

9 blocks

oak wood
planks

7 blocks

spruce wood
slab

END CHALLENGE PART 1

There are lots of valuable blocks and items that can only be found in the End dimension. And once you've defeated the dragon, the End is also fairly safe compared to the Overworld or the Nether, as there are far fewer hostile mobs to deal with. If you're ready for another challenge, let's set up a base in an End city so you can come and go whenever you like to collect the materials you need.

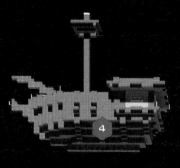

1: BRIDGES

Once you've defeated the dragon and travelled through the End gateway, use cobblestone blocks to build bridges between the islands or ender pearls to teleport across the gaps. Look for an End city – they're usually made up of several towers and an End ship. Remember to leave a trail of blocks from the portal to the city so you can always find your way back.

2: SHULKER ERADICATION

Clear the towers of shulkers. Use your sword to knock their projectiles off-course, and hit them when their shell is open to deal maximum damage. Keep water buckets in your inventory to break your fall if you're hit by a shulker projectile – you'll be inflicted with the levitation effect before dropping back down to the ground.

3: **SECURITY**

Add iron doors and switches to each tower entrance, then fill in the gap above the doorway with extra blocks. This will stop endermen and shulkers coming inside.

4: **LOOT**

Search all the towers for loot chests – you'll find everything from diamonds to horse armour. There are more chests in the ship, as well as an item frame containing elytra – wings that allow you to glide and will help you travel around more quickly.

END CHALLENGE PART 2

There aren't many sources of food in the End, but there is plenty of space to work with. You can bring materials over from the Overworld and use them to build a secure base, create all the equipment you need and set up several crop farms to provide you with a sustainable food source.

1: BASE

Create a partially-submerged base that's linked to one of the towers by digging down through the floor. Set up a crafting table, furnace, chest of supplies, ender chest to link back to the Overworld and equipment for brewing and enchanting. You can use the experience you earned defeating the dragon to enchant all your equipment. Remember not to add a bed as it will explode if you try to sleep in it.

2: CHICKEN FARM

 Creating an animal farm can be tricky as you'll need to push the animals through the End portal from the Overworld. But you can create a chicken coop quite easily – just bring plenty of eggs across and throw them into a pre-prepared enclosure. Approximately 1 in 8 will spawn a chicken when it hits the ground.

3: TREE FARM

You'll need plenty of wood for crafting, so set up a tree farm. Place dirt blocks in a square, add a glowstone border then plant some saplings and wait for them to grow. This will provide you with a renewable supply of saplings, wood and apples.

4: CROP FARM

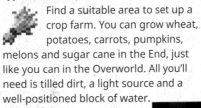 Find a suitable area to set up a crop farm. You can grow wheat, potatoes, carrots, pumpkins, melons and sugar cane in the End, just like you can in the Overworld. All you'll need is tilled dirt, a light source and a well-positioned block of water.

MINECRAFT STORY MODE

Story Mode is the newest way to play Minecraft. It's an action-packed, episodic adventure that you control through the main character, Jesse. Every decision you make will change the course of the story. Here's a spoiler-free intro, as well as some insider info from Mojang and Telltale Games.

You and your friends are huge fans of The Order of the Stone – Gabriel, Magnus, Ellegaard and Soren – a legendary group of Minecrafters who have slayed the ender dragon. But where are they? While at EnderCon, hoping to meet Gabriel the Warrior, it becomes clear that something is very wrong. Before long, terror is unleashed on the crowds and Gabriel asks for your help; he needs you to find Magnus and Ellegaard to help him stop the terror from destroying the world. There's no time to lose: Gabriel gives you an amulet which will guide you to Magnus and Ellegaard. You'll have many decisions to make during the course of your journey, and each decision will change the course of your adventure. Choose wisely!

MEET THE ORDER OF THE STONE

The characters bring Minecraft: Story Mode to life and drive the action and adventure. Here's a little more info about Jesse and the gang, and The Order of the Stone.

THE LEADER

JESSE

The leader of the gang and the playable character that you can customise to be either male or female. Loyal and kind to his or her friends, Jesse can get quite intense in heated situations.

Best quote
"NO MAN LEFT BEHIND. THAT'S MY MOTTO."

THE WARRIOR

GABRIEL

Considered by many to be the greatest warrior of his time. According to legend, Gabriel was the one who killed the dragon. He's brave and strong, and likes to help people.

Best quote
"SAY WHAT YOU LIKE ABOUT WITCHES, THEY SURE KNOW HOW TO MAKE A CAKE!"

THE REDSTONE ENGINEER

ELLEGAARD

Ellegaard is a redstone genius who has invented countless amazing and complicated devices. She's close friends with Soren the Architect but doesn't really get along with Magnus.

Best quote
"OH, YOU'RE STICKING UP FOR MAGNUS. THAT'S VERY ... SWEET."

Jesse and Reuben know you don't need a special outfit to be a hero, but Magnus does look pretty cool ...

Jesse and the gang find themselves everywhere from the Nether to the End during their adventures.

76 unique new skins were created, as well as 74 unique textures to create multiple variations.

THE ROGUE

MAGNUS

Magnus is very good at griefing and generally destroying things. He's also very smart and, despite his profession, honourable. He will always fight to help people out of trouble.

Best quote
"STOP EATING MY KINGDOM!"

THE TRADER

PETRA

Petra is a warrior and a trader. She has a knack for gathering resources and supplying them to others – for a price. She's tough and very protective of her friends so she's great to have on your side.

Best quote
"FOR THE RIGHT PRICE, I'LL HELP ANYONE."

THE PIG

REUBEN

Reuben is Jesse's pet pig and best friend. He's generally a happy pig and loves Jesse very much. He can be a little sensitive and gets upset with Jesse if he feels ignored.

Best quote
"OINK OINK."

THE BRAVE

AXEL

Axel is large and strong. He lives in the treehouse with Jesse and is very loyal to his friends, but also likes to play pranks on them. He's impulsive and not afraid to speak his mind.

Best quote
"ISN'T IT WEIRD HOW DISPENSERS ARE CARVED TO LOOK LIKE SPOOKY LITTLE FACES? WHAT DO YOU DISPENSE, LITTLE GUY?"

THE REDSTONE EXPERT

OLIVIA

Lives with Jesse and Axel. She's very smart and doesn't have much patience. She's good with redstone, and makes a daylight sensor for Reuben so that he won't be afraid at night.

Best quote
"WOULD YOU RATHER FIGHT A HUNDRED CHICKEN-SIZED ZOMBIES OR TEN ZOMBIE-SIZED CHICKENS?"

THE ARCHITECT

SOREN

The leader of The Order of the Stone and a great architect. He's considered the greatest builder, crafter and architect of all time, but he's been missing for years and nobody knows where he is.

Best quote
"STUFF AND NONSENSE, STUFF AND NONSENSE."

INSIDER INFO

Story Mode is full of Easter eggs – no, not the chocolate kind, inside jokes and references that are cleverly hidden so only the most observant will find them. Here are a couple – look out for more as you play.

You probably recognise the voices of the people who introduce Gabriel at EnderCon – yes, it's Lydia and Owen!

Jeb, lead developer for Minecraft, appears in the crowd at EnderCon. That's him with the red hair.

TNT MINER

Want to test your redstone skills and have a bit of fun at the same time? This TNT miner will blast a hole in the ground right down to the bedrock layer, simultaneously providing a shortcut to all those valuable ores and ample space for an underground base. Take a look at this exploded diagram showing how it's constructed, then check out the next page to see how it works.

⏱ 30 Mins ❶❷③④ EASY

1: DESIGN

The miner is built using stone and Nether brick and looks similar to a jungle temple.

2: HOLE

Once you've set the miner going, the resulting hole will be approximately 10 x 10 blocks, and as deep as the bedrock layer.

3: STORAGE

Chests can be placed at the side of the miner, so you can store extra TNT. You can also use the chests to store the valuable resources you mine, once you've blasted a hole down to the lower levels of the world.

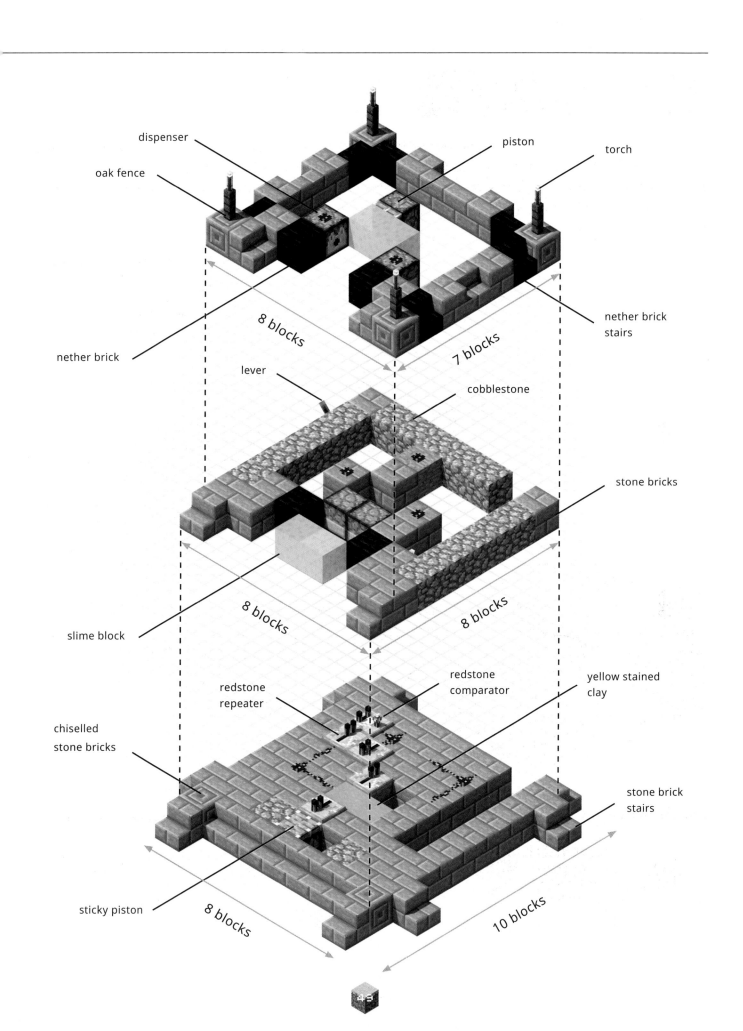

dispenser

oak fence

piston

torch

nether brick stairs

nether brick

8 blocks

7 blocks

lever

cobblestone

stone bricks

slime block

8 blocks

8 blocks

redstone repeater

redstone comparator

yellow stained clay

chiselled stone bricks

stone brick stairs

sticky piston

8 blocks

10 blocks

GETTING IT RIGHT

The redstone circuitry has to be exactly right for the TNT miner to work properly, and positioning is crucial if you don't want to blow up the entire build by accident. Follow the guidelines on this page and you'll be blasting your way down to the bedrock layer in no time.

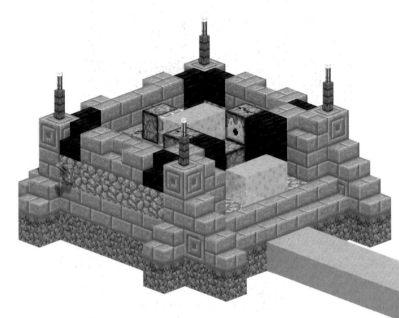

1: POSITIONING

 Position the front of the miner 10 blocks away from the area you'd like to mine. The miner will then blast a hole from sea level (y = 62) right down to the bedrock layer.

2: PREPARING THE AREA

Make sure you flatten and clear the area directly in front of the miner. This will stop the TNT blocks ricocheting back off trees or areas of higher ground and blowing up the miner. You can also place a water moat along the front as an added layer of protection – TNT won't detonate in water.

∃: PULSE CIRCUIT

The comparator and repeaters towards the back of the miner form what's known as a pulse circuit. A signal is continuously switched on and off, which is how the sticky pistons and the dispensers are powered. This is what keeps the TNT coming.

4: STICKY PISTONS AND SLIME BLOCKS

The sticky pistons push and pull the slime blocks. The TNT bounces off the slime blocks and is propelled forwards. The repeater at the front must be set to 3 ticks. 1, 2 or 4 ticks will result in the miner blowing itself up.

5: TNT AND DISPENSERS

Add the TNT to the dispensers last so you don't accidentally blow the miner up before you've finished. Fill each dispenser so that it's completely full (9 x 64-block stacks per dispenser), and the miner will run for around six and a half minutes.

Notch kicks things off in style, with the help of some streamers.

The ender dragon has found a new perch. Let's hope Big Ben can take the strain of Minecraft's most dangerous boss mob.

MINECON

MINECON is an epic convention for everyone who loves Minecraft. It's been going strong since 2011 and the crowds are getting bigger every year – people travel from all over the world to be part of the experience and meet the rest of the Minecraft community. Usually spread over two days, the schedule is packed with events.

Lydia receiving the award from the Guinness World Records adjudicator for largest crowd at a single game convention. MINECON is officially amazing!

Mojang presenting a cheque to the Make-A-Wish Foundation.

Minecraft: bringing people together since 2011.

The costume competition is always highly competitive, and this epic red dragon is a particularly worthy contender.

A packed Qcraft demo – even the creepers want to know what it's about.

There are panels hosted by Mojang and popular YouTubers, exhibits and gaming areas, stalls where you can check out the latest Minecraft merch and workshops to help you master the trickier elements of the game. There are also parties where you can meet other members of the community. Oh, and there's a costume competition where you can showcase your creative talents.

MINECON is well-known for its impressive exhibits. This London-themed park and road were the talk of the town in 2015.

MINECON's oldest attendee, Selma, celebrating her 98th birthday at MINECON!

An epic rollercoaster at the Islands of Adventure party.

MINECON

MINECON is held in a different location across the globe every year. Well, it's only fair, right? From Las Vegas in 2011 to London in 2015, check out some of the highlights from previous MINECONS – they're sure to get you in the mood for California 2016!

MINECON 2013

Location: Orlando, Florida

Everyone was very excited about the Qcraft demo – a mod that brings the principles of quantum physics to Minecraft and is used as an educational tool in classrooms. The LEGO Minecraft figures were also very popular. There was an Islands of Adventure Party. The costume competition was particularly competitive. And MINECON's oldest participant turned 98 on the day of the closing ceremony.

CAPE

Attendees: 7,500

MINECON 2011

Location: Mandalay Bay, Las Vegas

The very first MINECON celebrated the release of Minecraft 1.0 – the official version of the game – for PC. Notch gave the keynote speech in honour of this. There was a Nether party, featuring Deadmau5, for over-21s. Mojang donated $20,000 to the Make-A-Wish Foundation. And there was a marriage proposal! And she said yes!

CAPE

Attendees: 5,000

MINECON 2012

Location: Disneyland, Paris

CAPE

The redstone update was announced during the keynote speech. The subsequent redstone talk was so popular that most people couldn't get in. Notch did a panel event. CaptainSparklez debuted his video 'Minecraft-Style'. Hat Films did a panel event to explain how they started making films. There was a secret party featuring Skrillex and a costume competition.

Attendees: 6,500

MINECON 2015

Location: London, England

CAPE

The 2015 London MINECON broke the world record for the largest crowd at a single game convention. The Story Mode trailer debuted during the opening ceremony. Later, Mojang and Telltale Games gave a talk about their upcoming plans for the spin-off game. There were various London-themed exhibits, including an enormous Big Ben statue complete with ender dragon. An epic build battle took place between Dan TDM and Vikkstar123 and Stampy and Sqaishey. Egmont's book stand had a block pit which proved to be very popular with children and adults alike. There was a live show on the first evening. And, of course, there was the traditional costume competition.

Attendees: 10,000

BEST AND WORST DAYS IN MINECRAFT: YOUTUBER EDITION

Just like you, your favourite YouTubers have had good days in Minecraft, when everything has gone their way, and bad days when nothing has gone right and things have ended in disaster. Here's what FyreUK, Stampy Cat and AmyLee33 had to say about their best and worst days.

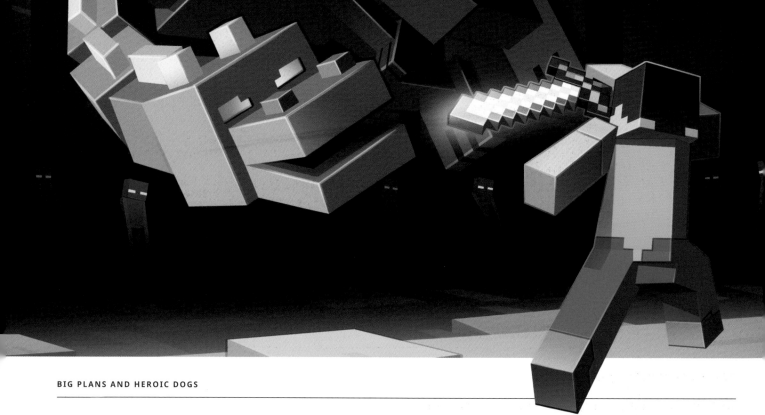

BIG PLANS AND HEROIC DOGS

STAMPY CAT

BEST DAY I was exploring on my very first day, and I was just starting to experiment with crafting when the sun set. I dug into a mountain to make a cave, then tried to sleep. A zombie and a spider attacked me but I defeated them. While I waited for daylight I planned how I wanted my house to look and how I could make it safe. At that moment I realised the potential of Minecraft and how much time I was going to spend playing this game.

WORST DAY I'd been playing for about a month and I was out and about, gathering wood with my first dog, Gregory – he went everywhere with me. It started to get dark so I began to make my way home, but I wasn't fast enough and googlies began spawning all around us. I had plenty of armour so I wasn't worried when I got shot by an arrow from a skeleton. Gregory, however, charged after the skeleton, and sadly died in his efforts to protect me. I had a funeral for him and planted a tree in his memory. I have had many dogs since Gregory, but none of them have been the same.

AMYLEE33

BEST DAY It was the day I got my first dogs! I headed out for an adventure in the desert and found my first desert temple. After collecting the loot – gold, iron, rotten flesh and bones – I headed home through a taiga biome where I managed to tame two wolves. I called one Lexi and asked my viewers to name the other – they chose Max. Years later I still have them – they're my oldest dogs.

WORST DAY I had found an amazing cave and mined my first diamonds – eight of them – and an emerald! I even tackled a zombie spawner and lived. I came across a huge lava pit, but I didn't have a bucket of water so I decided not to explore any further. As I was making my way out, a creeper began to walk towards me, hissing, so I backed away to get some distance. Unfortunately I forgot about the lava pit and fell straight into it. The creeper just stared at me the whole time – I think he planned it.

FYREUK – CREATIVE BUILDING TEAM

BEST DAY It was the day we finished our first big build as a team back in the summer of 2011. We had over sixty people working on a huge train station. We created the entire building as well as interior details like a departure board, a waiting area and, of course, several large trains. We recorded the process and turned it into a timelapse video for our YouTube channel – it even attracted the attention of Notch who mentioned it on social media.

WORST DAY There have been several occasions when fires have spread through our wooden towns and cities, causing huge amounts of destruction – luckily we made backups. Mojang eventually added a command to stop fire spreading, and since then none of our constructions have burned down.

RARE BLOCKS AND ITEMS

Minecraft's most valuable blocks and items are often the rarest and most difficult to get hold of in Survival mode. Knowing where to look is half the battle, and with these handy tips for how to retrieve them you'll soon be the proud owner of each and every material on this page.

DRAGON EGG

Rarity:
One per world (found in the End), this is Minecraft's rarest block.
Why you want it:
For bragging rights. It's a trophy that proves you're awesome enough to have defeated the ender dragon.
How to get it:
Once you've defeated the ender dragon you'll need to use pistons to push the egg off the portal as a collectible item. Do not mine it or you will lose it.

GHAST TEAR

Rarity:
Nether-dwelling ghasts may drop a single tear when they die. If you're lucky. Although they may drop it into lava.
Why you want it:
You need ghast tears to make mundane potion and potion of regeneration.
How to get it:
Take out a ghast, ideally with an enchanted bow, and not while the ghast is flying over lava, then hope it drops one.

MAGMA CREAM

Rarity:
Large and medium magma cubes have a 25% chance of dropping 1 magma cream when they die.
Why you want it:
You'll need magma cream to make mundane potion and potion of fire resistance.
How to get it:
Use a looting sword to kill magma cubes and the chance of them dropping magma cream will increase.

WITHER SKELETON SKULL

Rarity:
There's a 2.5% chance of a wither skeleton dropping one when killed by a player or a tamed wolf.
Why you want it:
To get 3 wither skeleton skulls so you can craft the wither, which is the only way you can get a Nether star.
How to get it:
Using a looting sword increases the chance of wither skeletons dropping a skull.

ELYTRA

Rarity:
In End cities, one pair of elytra can be found in an item frame in each End ship.
Why you want it:
When equipped in your chestplate slot elytra allow you to glide through the air.
How to get it:
You'll need to defeat the ender dragon then make your way through the portal to an End city – you'll find them in an item frame in the treasure room of the ship.

NETHER STAR

Rarity:
Very rare. The wither will drop 1 Nether star when it dies, but it's very difficult to kill the wither.
Why you want it:
Without a Nether star you won't be able to craft beacon blocks, which are essential to make power pyramids – structures that give you power boosts.
How to get it:
You'll need a solid plan to defeat the wither and a complete set of enchanted diamond equipment.

EMERALD ORE

Rarity:
Only found in extreme hills biomes, between levels 4 and 32, and only ever in single blocks.
Why you want it:
When mined it drops an emerald, which you can use to craft solid blocks of emerald or to trade with villagers.
How to get it:
Get mining in an extreme hills biome. When you find it, mine it with a fortune pickaxe and it could drop up to 4 emeralds.

BOTTLE O' ENCHANTING

Rarity:
They're sold by villager clerics, for 3-11 emeralds, in their fourth tier of trading.
Why you want it:
When thrown, a bottle o' enchanting will provide you with 3-11 experience points, which will come in handy.
How to get it:
Find your nearest NPC village and track down a purple-robed cleric. Keep trading with him until he offers you a bottle o' enchanting.

DRAGON HEAD

Rarity:
Dragon heads can only be found on the bow of End ships in End cities.
Why you want it:
To prove that you made it to an End city, and for decoration – it can be mounted on a wall and powered by redstone so that it opens and closes its mouth.
How to get it:
Go to the End, defeat the ender dragon, then make your way to an End city on the outer islands and locate a ship.

FESTIVE NPC VILLAGE

If you've come across an NPC village during your Minecraft adventures, you'll know how helpful the local villagers can be. This festive season, why not give something back? Spread the cheer and help them celebrate in style by treating the entire village to a fun, festive makeover.

BEFORE

1: TREE

Make a tree out of spruce wood and leaves. Use glowstone for lights, single fence posts and coloured blocks for baubles, then top it off with a glowstone star. Use different combinations of coloured blocks to create some interesting parcels underneath.

2: WALLS

Build walls around the village and line them with regular torches and redstone torches. Use snow and redstone blocks to create a festive candy cane effect along the top.

3: NUTCRACKER GUARDS

Add an entry point to your walls (iron doors with switches will keep hostile mobs out), then build two nutcrackers to stand guard either side of the entrance. See the next page for an exploded diagram.

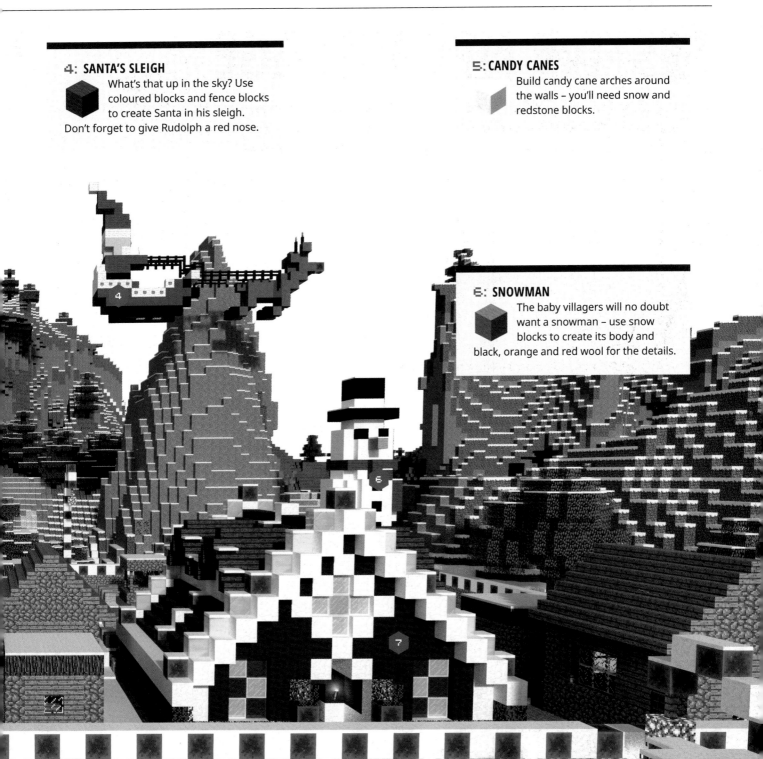

4: SANTA'S SLEIGH
What's that up in the sky? Use coloured blocks and fence blocks to create Santa in his sleigh. Don't forget to give Rudolph a red nose.

5: CANDY CANES
Build candy cane arches around the walls – you'll need snow and redstone blocks.

6: SNOWMAN
The baby villagers will no doubt want a snowman – use snow blocks to create its body and black, orange and red wool for the details.

7: CANDY COTTAGE
Build the outline of a candy cottage using brown stained clay and snow, then use solid blocks of ore to add coloured sweet details. See the next page for an exploded diagram.

FESTIVE NPC VILLAGE

You'll want to pay special attention to the nutcracker guards and the candy cottage, to make sure they look just right. Take a look at these exploded diagrams to see exactly how they're put together, or use them as inspiration and have fun creating your own designs.

NUTCRACKER GUARD

⏱ 35 MINS ⬡1 ⬡ ⬡ ⬡ BEGINNER

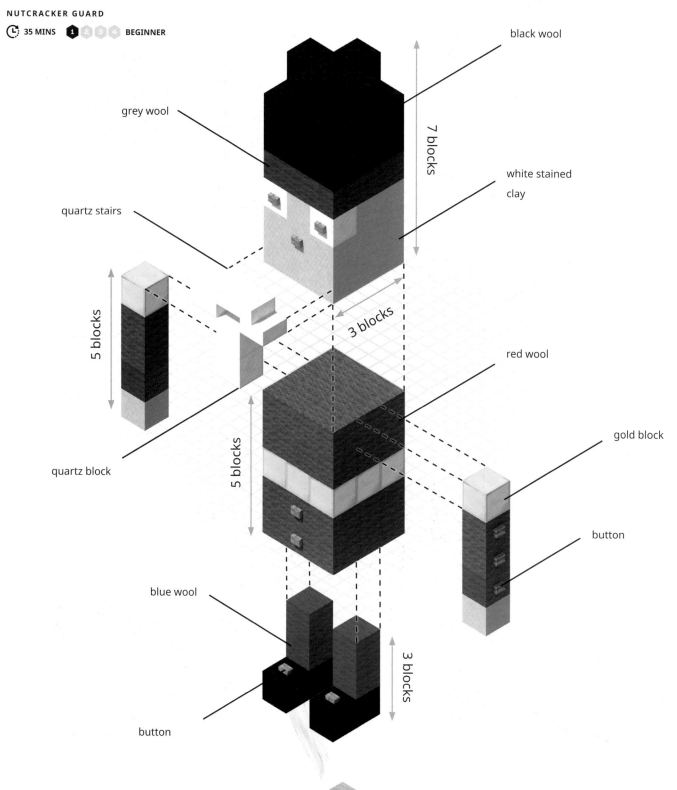

black wool

grey wool

7 blocks

white stained clay

quartz stairs

5 blocks

3 blocks

red wool

gold block

quartz block

5 blocks

button

blue wool

3 blocks

button

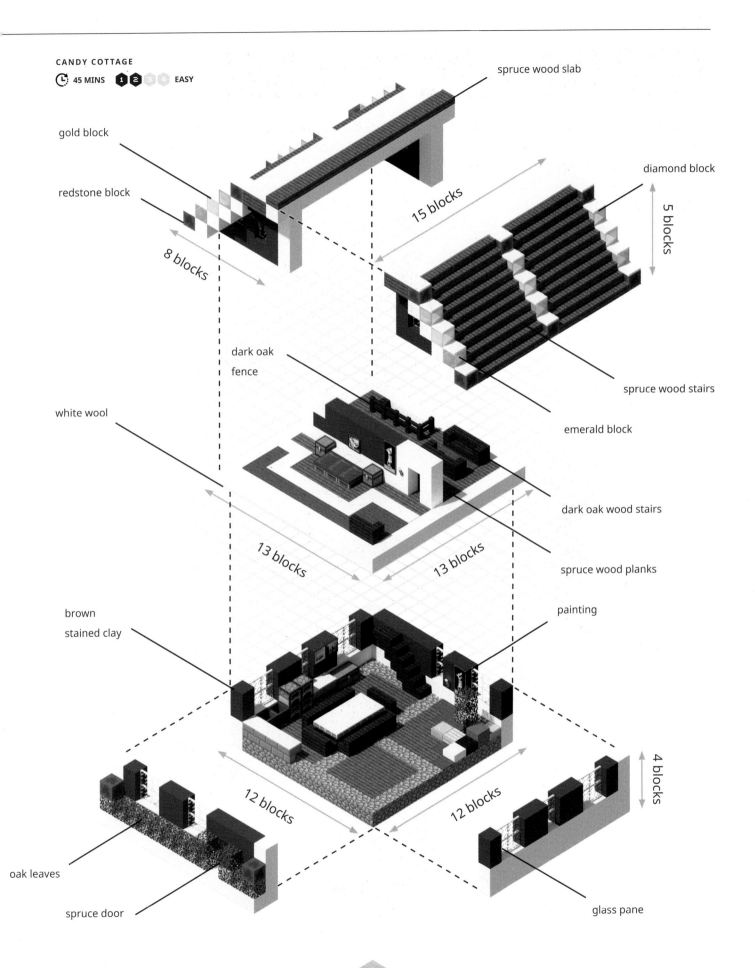

CANDY COTTAGE

⏱ 45 MINS 1 2 3 4 EASY

spruce wood slab

gold block

redstone block

diamond block

5 blocks

8 blocks

15 blocks

dark oak fence

spruce wood stairs

white wool

emerald block

dark oak wood stairs

spruce wood planks

13 blocks

13 blocks

brown stained clay

painting

oak leaves

spruce door

12 blocks

12 blocks

4 blocks

glass pane

OFFICIAL LOOT

Not all treasures need to be sought deep underground – you can find plenty of precious loot right here on this page! Declare your love for Minecraft with a bold tee, stack your shelves with collectible characters, or snuggle with a plush while you swot up on Blockopedia facts.

TOYS

MEDICOM BE@RBRICK SERIES 31
Something about this bear suggests it might have a short fuse. Medicom have been making Be@rbricks since 2001 and have created this creeper-themed bear in honour of Minecraft. Other featured designs have been by the likes of H R Giger and Vivienne Westwood. Fancy!

I PORKCHOP MINECRAFT TEE

Express your passion with a scrumptious porky snack.

STEVE THE MINER TEE

Wear this and inspire yourself to dig for victory!

CAREER OPPORTUNITIES TEE

So many ways to play! Keep your options open with this tee.

IRON GOLEM TEE

Conjure up this tough ally. No pumpkin required!

GLIMPSE TEE

Look carefully! What you see may just leave you aghast.

CREEPER ANATOMY TEE

Discover the darkness that lies within a creeper's heart!

RUMOUR HAS IT TEE

Celebrate this slimy union of tendrilled sweethearts.

OWNER OF THE SPHERE TEE

Round out your look with this fish-eye illustration.

HILLTOP BY CAPY TEE

Take the high ground in any fashion dispute.

ANIMAL TOTEM TEE

Cuboid livestock: cute, delicious and easily stacked.

POWERED BY REDSTONE TEE

You're a mighty machine! Just take care around TNT.

CREEPER INSIDE TEE

Are creepers as close to your heart as they are to ours?

FOAM DIAMOND SWORD

Swing the bling with this durable foam sword.

FOAM DIAMOND PICKAXE

Get cracking in spectacular style with this flashy foam tool.

FOAM IRON SWORD

Mobs will quail in fear before your mighty (squishy) blade.

FOAM STONE PICKAXE

The essential tool, if a little spongier than normal.

DIAMOND STEVE VINYL

Strike a pose with this figure of Steve in his finest gear.

CREEPER ANATOMY DELUXE VINYL FIGURE

See what keeps creepers ticking with this scientific slice-up!

STEVE VINYL FIGURE

Can you dig it? Steve can! Prove it with this poseable figure.

CREEPER VINYL FIGURE

A fearsome figurine for your shelf. Nervous around cats.

PIG-TO-PORK-CHOP PLUSH CHARACTER

Turn this adorable beast inside out to reveal a meaty treat!

ZOMBIE PIGMAN PLUSH

From the depths of the Nether to the depths of your heart.

GHAST PLUSH

No need to cry. Comfort this monstrosity with a hug.

COW-TO-RAW BEEF PLUSH CHARACTER

A reversible plush that is as delicious as it is cuddlesome.

MINECRAFT: THE COMPLETE HANDBOOK COLLECTION

Learn to build, create, and explore with these guides.

MINECRAFT BLOCKOPEDIA

All the info, from cobblestone to precious prismarine.

STEVE HEAD

Transform into Minecraft's most notorious blockhead.

CREEPER HEAD

That'sssss a very nice disguise you've got there ...

MINI COLLECTOR CASE

Take a little bit of Minecraft with you wherever you go.

ENDERMAN VINYL

The enderman may strike fear in the hearts of men, but this little guy promises not to terrorise the neighbourhood as long as he has a block to hold and a noble place to stand in your room or office.

Just make sure that visitors know the enderman can be a bit shy, and that it's rude to stare!

IRON GOLEM PLUSH

This solemn protector will repel mobs and deliver hugs.

TEST YOUR MINECRAFT KNOWLEDGE

How well do you think you know Minecraft? Really? That well? OK, if you're up for the challenge, take this tricky quiz and find out how much of an expert you actually are. No cheating!

1. You're about to go exploring. Draw the recipe for a compass in the crafting grid below.

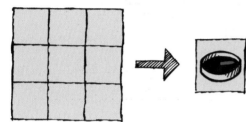

2. Can you work out which mob has just died from the items it has dropped? Write your answer below.

GUNPOWDER   REDSTONE DUST   STICKS

....

3. The creeper was invented by accident, due to a programming error that occurred whilst Notch was creating another mob. Which mob was Notch trying to create?

....

4. Which of the following items might you find in a desert temple chest? Tick the correct items.

 ☐   ☐   ☐   ☐

BONE   SAND   SPIDER EYE   REDSTONE DUST

 ☐   ☐   ☐   ☐

BREAD   COAL   GOLD HORSE ARMOUR   DIAMOND

5. Minecraft maps are divided into 16 x 16 x 128 block sections. What are these sections called?

....

6. What kind of villager does this trading screen belong to? Write your answer below.

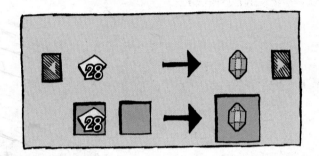

....

7. This daylight sensor recipe is incomplete. Write the name of the missing ingredient, then draw it into the crafting grid below.

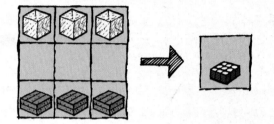

....

8. You're about to eat a pumpkin pie. Colour in the number of food points it will restore.

9. How would you arrange bookshelves around an enchantment table to maximise the power of the table? Draw them in the grid below.

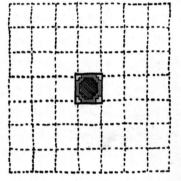

10. What status boost do each of the following power pyramid symbols represent? Write the answer underneath each symbol.

....

....

....

11. What is the name of the person who created the soundtrack for Minecraft?

....

12. What was Minecraft originally called?

....

ANSWERS ON PAGE 71

GOODBYE!

You've reached the end of the 2017 Minecraft Annual. Congratulations!

We hope you've enjoyed every single word and picture. Thanks for playing Minecraft, and extra thanks for reading about it.

Adventure bravely into the new year and craft yourself a great 2017!

Owen Hill,
Mojang

ANSWERS

1.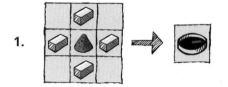

2. A witch

3. A pig

4.

BONE SAND SPIDER EYE GOLD HORSE DIAMOND
ARMOUR

5. Chunks

6. A librarian

7. Nether quartz

8.

9.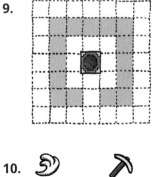

10.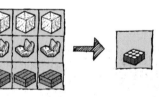

SPEED HASTE RESISTANCE JUMP BOOST

11. C418

12. Cave Game

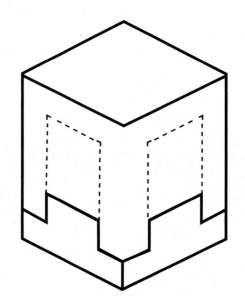